# PLUNK

# PLUNK

## Tom C. Hunley

WSC PRESS

**Plunk**
by Tom Hunley
Copyright © 2015

ISBN: 978-0-9910139-2-0

$16.00

Cover design by Tyisha Wrice
Layout design by Dustin Riggins

WSC Press
1111 Main Street
Wayne, NE 68787
wscpress@wsc.edu
www.wscpress.com

# Contents

*momentarily we're floating
like needles on water.*

—Dean Young, "May Deaths"

# PLUNK

## Um

Often I'm awakened by awful noises:
jackhammers, dynamite, walls crumbling
and bigger ones climbing the sky
in their places. My future arrives and I
have to settle for it. I don't understand how
I got here any more than a lobster understands
how it ended up in a tank next to a *Please wait*
*to be seated* sign, but both of us can read
the faces of the cruelly beautiful women
pointing at us. I always feel eyes on me,
so I apologize to insects after I kill them
and to the salmon on my plate, caught
being nostalgic for home. Everything looks clear
if you squint just right, and at least once a day
I realize that whatever I've been saying
isn't the point at all. I spend most days listening
to other people almost making sense, and I don't
ask them what the hell they're talking about
because they're on television or the radio or
because I'm eavesdropping from the next table.
When I'm not talking or listening, I'm in a
boil, my shell softening. I'm getting a good look
at a wrecking ball. I'm crumbling.
I volunteered for all this, accidentally,
by raising my hand, intending to ask
a question I couldn't put into words.

## What Can be Said about the Beautiful-from-a-Distance Elegant Etcetera in the Broken Syllables of our Imperfect Tongues?

In our lust for lists and our need
to name, what sense there is
to be made gets made and unmade
like a bed, and we are both
the despairing maid and the young boy,
ecstatic to have tousled it
into a senseless mess like strewn wildflowers
he would bouquet for her if he
were older. Umbrella eaves and
the darkening of sky, we contain both
of these, the little black-keyed symphony
that begins with a note of despair
and ends with heartcries of flesh
and longing and morning after sighs
and the great convulsive sadness of knowing
that we never could love as we should love.
I have been spared the unspeakable sufferings
that the newspapers shout out daily,
so I can't truly know the greatest joys
and gratitudes, and I'm grateful not to know.
I'll buy you flowers before you're buried
in posthumous praise.  Casting its light
in this beautiful park, the sun rests on
our skin. Nothing more remarkable has ever happened.
Home is where the heart attack is.
I'll buy you a drink before one of us,
in our clumsy fumbling, breaks.
The heart attack wants what the heart attack wants.
I have been singing happy songs
into your mouth for the mere pleasure
of listening when you lift them
back to my ears, those ditches
where so many silly voices have dumped

so many silly words. The maid, tired
from scouring other people's houses, spanked
the spoiled rich boy silly and his parents fired her,
their blue blood boiling. A hinge that opened the door
to a better life, it turned out, for it forced her
to go to college, get an MBA, become a CEO.
If you're wondering whether their paths
crossed again, that's good, wonder being
central to poetry. Anyone who has ever
felt nervous or awkward in a crowd but comforted
to learn it's only part of some larger nervousness
spreading in the crowd like The Wave, or any scarred body
that has ever felt marred beyond hope of beauty, lodged
in a bottle, lost in an antidepressant fog yet still praising
naked infinite possibility knows what I'm talking about.
The swervings of the heart. The remarkable change
of the sky from hour to hour. That sort of thing.
The spoiled boy-turned humble man
and the maid-turned CEO did find each other
and they married, but their marriage belly-flopped.
She married the idea of all the unfairness
in this world under her thumb, over her lap.
He married the memory of someone caring enough
to correct his course. Their marriage died of a heart attack.
Wherever you go, they are there, the luckless in love.
I can taste them on your tongue, answers to a question
I won't let myself ask. I kiss you harder as if to insist
that the boy didn't jump on the bed when the maid
told him not to, and I will never leave you, neither of us
will have a heart attack, ever, the sun resting
on our skin will never depart, leaving us cold in the dark,
and as for the black keys on the piano,
the minor notes, the weepy tones,
we'll pry them right off the keyboard.

## Moonhandled

An 80-year-old woman enters Steak N'Shake,
orders black coffee, and beeps like Roadrunner
every time she needs a refill. The waitress sees
the surprise in my eyes, leans in, says, *Hon,*
*she comes in here every full moon without fail.*

The waitress's face is the wrinkled map
of one of those places everyone visits but no one
lives in. She makes me fall in love with her
loneliness, or maybe that's the moon. The
old woman beeps, bangs her empty cup

on the bar. I think I hear a coyote
among the wind-rattled trash cans.
The waitress and I agree that it's a lunatic world.
The day's headlines confirm it: *Thieves Lift*
*Occupied Porta-potty! Hostage Fired for Missing Work!*

She tells me about her son competing with
his college roommate over who could spit farthest
out their dorm window. The roommate thought
a running start would propel his spit a record distance,
but he tumbled out the window and landed before

the spit, which hit his face. *Full moon,* says
the waitress, *but he survived, and maybe it was*
*the booze, not the moon, that made him do it.* I tell her
about Li Po, who got drunk, tried to embrace
the moon's reflection in a lake, passed out,

and drowned. *Maybe the moon is really messing with us,*
I tell her. *Just in case,* I say, *let's take our biggest*
*rockets and knock it down.* She laughs.
I head for the lake, where I catch the moon
floating like a fat, pasty tourist

bobbing in an inner tube. I throw a rock at it
and yell "leave us alone!" But then a vision of
the world without the moon flashes, like
someone else's life, before my eyes, and it
looks something like *Invasion of the Body Snatchers*:

everyone the same, no one very interesting. Dear Lady,
those are my yellowed claws scratching your door,
that's my howl, my scritch, my faint siren in the night,
and this is my mange, my tangle of hair everywhere,
my belly itching for the ends of your nails.

## Speechless Like Michael Caine

If it's true that the core of the Milky Way
smells like raspberries and tastes like rum,
as astronomer Arnaud Belloche says,
and if it's true that every pomegranate
everywhere contains exactly 285 seeds
— or maybe 263 but anyway Kelsey says
they all have the same amount —
and if it's really true that our earlobes
align perfectly with our nipples, as Katie says,
well then I'm stunned, mouth agape, like
Michael Caine on the set of *Batman*, struck dumb
upon first sight of Heath Ledger as The Joker.
"What's my first line?  What's my first line?"
Michael Caine, playing Alfred, must have wondered,
fumbling for the line like a poet or like me
when I first saw you, across the room
at a party.  I'd like to say I was cool
like Brando, in *Streetcar*, "We've had this date
from the beginning," but that would be untrue.
I was tongue-tied, speechless like Michael Caine.
If it's true that 100,000 Jews escaped Sweden
the night before the Nazis arrived because
citizens with boats rallied to ferry them away
— and why doubt it?  The stars are evidence
that bright lights interrupt the sprawling darkness —
then maybe I can believe that astronomers,
if they squinted hard enough, could see
our love and smell it and taste it and chart it
on the stars, which also predict with some certainty
that you'll never leave me and we'll
never leave this miraculous life.

## Permanent

*Hey, your tattoo fell off,* I said, and picked it up,
but she thought I was trying to pick her up,
so she rushed away, her legs long and tan except
for a balloon-shaped vacancy on her ankle where
the tattoo had rented space. She was beautiful with
curly hair and probably men had been hitting on her
for as long as she could remember, and maybe she
assumed that fending off their attentions would be
a permanent part of her life. Listen, my parents died
last year. They were always there, hovering,
when I was small. First the air went out
of their marriage, and then Pop was gone, and after that,
Mom was gone, and a little while after that, I made up
that preposterous story about the woman whose tattoo
fell off, I guess to illustrate something about impermanence.
I should have just said that in Seattle, circa 1991, I saw
a Blood or maybe a Crip with a tattoo of a tear under
his eye. Since then, the Bloods and Crips have gone legit.
They own their own record labels, plus a nightclub or two
in Rainier Valley and a majority share in Tully's Coffee.
A work crew dynamited the Kingdome in 2000,
and Mt. Rainier is an active volcano, so even it
won't stand forever, and I haven't lived
in my home town for fifteen years, but that woman
I started to tell you about, she poured her whole self
into an embrace with this scuzzball of my acquaintance.
Good woman finds bad man and gets lost.
That theme is a fixture on Lifetime and Oxygen.
I shouldn't have made that up about my parents dying
or about the gangs trafficking in coffee. I wanted,
I guess, to show you something about impermanence.
I wanted, ironically, to make a lasting impression
on the subject. I should have just led with the fact
that the old Rainier Brewery is now the headquarters
for Tully's Coffee. If a landmark like that can't last,

maybe no one's marriage has a chance; maybe all of us
should tattoo tears beneath our eyes or fill our hearts
with helium and reckless love and let them fly
untethered and brightly-colored across the sky.

## Wives of the Poets

Last week I told my class how Elinor Frost never forgave Robert
for little Elliot's death. She thought he didn't alert medics fast enough.
*Maybe he took the road with too much traffic,*
cracked a bearded, bespectacled young man,
*or got lost in the beauty of the woods.*
*How can you joke about them losing a child?*
accused a young woman with long earrings and boots,
and we launched into "Home Burial."

Flip a quarter and it's either an eagle flying
away as fast as it can or a dead president
trying to look dignified despite the worms
under his wig. This week I tell them
Wallace Stevens said *A poet looks at the world*
*the way a man looks at a woman*, but he
and his wife, Elsie, lived in separate sections of their house
and he never wrote her a love poem.
*Thirteen ways of looking at a jackass*,
murmurs the young woman, arms and brows crossed,
and the young man replies, *I'll bet he got tired of her*
*getting on his case when he just wanted to unwind*
*with a little Guitar Hero*, and I say, *We don't know*
*much about his life, but...*

It's fall semester, and as the trees bare themselves, the students
cover up and take back all the promises of spring
as the hot kisses they've planted on each other
ice over, and I know that next week when I tell them about
Williams Carlos Williams cheating on his wife, Flossie, these two
will say, *So much depends upon you flirting with my roommate*,
and *Not ideas about the cheapskate but the cheapskate himself.*

Today you broke the garage door and said *I'm sorry.*
You let the laundry pile up, and you're sorry.
Here I am airing our dirty laundry. I'm sorry,

you married a writer. All day I've planned my classes
and now I'm far away from you, lost in the woods of this poem,
which isn't great or maybe even good, and I'm sorry
that literary biographers and classrooms in the future
probably won't be discussing our marriage.
We're a sorry couple and no longer young,
but flip a coin a hundred times, and fifty times you'll forgive me,
and fifty times I'll tell you there's nothing to forgive.

## Psalm on a Theme by Dean Young and a Somewhat Similar Theme by Allen Ginsberg

When I die, Lord, I want to come back
as a cloud an airplane passes through
just before the crash,
lit up by blazing sunset
and just freed of a heavy, cleansing rain—
a cloud gifted with speech
enough to say *Change your course, pilot.*
I want to change, cloudlike,
into the sort of person who finds a wallet
and an abandoned infant and knows which to keep,
which to return, and does it. Sometimes I lose myself
in a crowd. Sometimes I find myself
in a cloud. Sometimes I want to die, Lord,
from embarrassment. An expression
like *I'm falling apart* or *I love you to pieces,*
but if I do fall apart, Lord, I do
want you to love me to pieces.
It is written in a Dean Young poem,
*The mind is a tiny island you've washed upon.*
Is that true, Lord? About me, not you, I mean.
Dean Young the poet, not Dean Young the creator
of the comic strip, *Blondie*, I mean.
Allen Ginsberg wrote, *I'm sick of my own mind.*
Give me just a little piece of yours, Lord.
*I'm going to give you a piece of my mind*
is an expression, but I mean it literally.
*I feel like a sandwich* is an expression
meaning I crave bread and cheese
with ham/lettuce/mustard if you please,
but sometimes I do feel like Dagwood has
his eyes then his hands then his drooling mouth on me
and I feel like I know how Blondie must feel.
This makes me realize I don't want to die.
I've wandered forty years through the desert

of my mind, Lord. I want you to fill my mouth
with water and prayer and maybe a jagged little song.

## Another Dream of Falling

Potato chip-colored old man, I don't know you
or where you pedaled your bicycle as I
drove by, just as birds don't know anything
of the pockets of air they fly past. We were
on Main Street in Osage, Iowa. I was driving
to see a dying relative for the last time. You
were thin and bald, and in your green windbreaker
you reminded me of a turtle. Driving on was like
turning a page and watching one story become
another. Outside Sioux Falls, I saw a white car
so dirt-packed I couldn't read the license plate,
the way I can't tell time in my sleep. Later I saw
some cows lazing in front of a "Wear Fur" sign.
I forgot my name and wished I knew yours
as the sun hit the pavement before setting.
I slept in a hotel bed, listened to the sound of
my own breathing, dreamed of flying and then falling.
I dreamed of the broad curves of Crazy Woman
Creek Road, which I had driven down days before
as the sky hazed over. I dreamed of dying
but it was like a turtle entering water, the water
creasing and then smoothing itself out. Your eyes
had met mine for a second, and I could have sworn
that something passed between us, as if you
tossed a skipping stone through my window
and it landed flat in my hand.

**Speaking of Falls,**

last year's arrived like a stone
from a slingshot.
Paintings awoke on our walls.
One song followed another and then another
until the sun went down like weak tea
and we couldn't speak.
Not to mention the cocky superheroes,
Beelzebub's ballerinas and princesses,
and the Plutonian SpongeBobs
all begging and booing and asking us
to smell their dirty little feet
as if we looked to them like candy
wrappers strewn across a lawn.
*Trick or treat* said the beers to our stomachs.
And when the darkness finally crescendoed,
we withered and shriveled and fell.
And then the guitars broke us as always
and we lurched into city buses
like stones skipping across a pond just before
plunk. And the loneliness that blew through us
was not even our own.

## What If There Lives, Within You, A Man Who Loves Random Consolations?

If the sun pinks his skin all over, he says *yeah*
*but night has come, the sun has conceded,*
*I win.* What if, deep inside your ears,
you can hear this man making the rounds
in his tiny secret townhouse? He tells your sick
lungs *at least you're still breathing,* and he tells
your heart *kudos on remembering to beat even*
*at night in a sleeping body of (mostly) water.*
What if he gets a toothache and says *at least*
*I have teeth?* Says *I never noticed them before?*
He might embarrass you. You might hide him
behind that mask you wear which is becoming
your face. He might feel jilted. He might try to change
for you or let you change him, the way big rocks
on the beach let gulls paint them guano-white,
anything to have some company other than
the vast ocean whose roar sounds like an endless
dial tone. He might turn rabid, a threat in the shadows.
Then who will encourage the teeth in your mouth
to hang in there? Who will cheer on your
white blood cells? *You made me human,*
you begin to tell him, but then you die
before you get to finish. You no longer remember
the time your house caught fire, how a strange voice
from deep inside said *hey, at least now*
*you don't have to wash those dishes,*
*and yay, here comes the ice cream man, carrying*
*a little song and a whole truck full*
*of goodness that those flames haven't melted.*

## At the Afterlife Bar and Grill

A glass falls and fills the clouds with shards,
a broken window through which we still see
the beforeworld, magnified
so we almost think we can go back.
A kitten mewing in a woodpile.
A child lost on the street. A mother, panicked
at the police station, her lucky penny tossed
down the wrong well. We can't do anything
but watch and maybe, finally, get to know
our neighbors. The world was Eden after all,
but after dark, before fire. We never could see
the great Godzilla, but something smelled awful
and our friends kept getting stepped on.
Over a drink, we remember cold nights that froze
our beards. Over another, we recall how sharing
a cigarette was the closest we got most nights to sharing
each other's breath, how we believed
that sleep and wakefulness were different states.
That *I love you* and *fuck off* were antonyms.
Alive, we could never find the right words,
blind dates who said they'd come right back but didn't.
The barmaid's an angel, and the low yowl of Mozart
and Mingus's latest jam rises from the juke box
like a body from a tomb. Alive, I was a radio
that lost reception.  There were miracles
everywhere, on earth as it is in heaven,
but my eyes were union workers on their lunch break.
These hot wings are miracles, but everything's a miracle.
You say, *let me tell you something in confidence.*
Your voice climbs onto some ledge
that my ears can't walk you off of.
You say *I can't handle all these miracles.*
You drink until you fall down because
it's way too much for you to stand.

## Heretical Gospel with Beer and Peanut Shells

No one believes in God
these days, lamented God,
the words dripping through my
ready pen, dictated, I swear
to God, who went on to say
He understands, He's had
His own share of self-doubt,
wondering if the light He made
was too bright. You try making
something beautiful without practicing
a whole lot first, He told Adam.
Maybe I wrote it wrong.
This happened so long ago.
So much has happened since:
the straining under too much weight,
the hair today gone tomorrow,
the marriage of the rock to the window.
Now I feel like a cat with paws declawed,
my creditors have got my number,
and a boxer on the sports bar TV
punches until he can't stand
the pain. Someone spat peanut shells
onto the floor and someone else's
bottle of Amber Bock lies spilling on
the counter, mortally-wounded soldier.
The fog on the street feels safe,
though it is alone, and somewhere
a neon light cuts through, a sign.
An exit finds someone willing
to walk through it before it slams shut
with a thud and for good.

## More Than One Cup of Gas Station Coffee

Some mornings the sky turns into
a big dark threat like my third
grade teacher spanking her palm red
with a ruler, measuring the fear
in our eyes and our ability to pay
quiet attention. When did I change
from a squirming tangle of energy
into a still alive thing, a conscious
rock that needs to be lifted and flung
in order to get anywhere? If I've learned
anything from zombie films, it's that
sentimentality will kill you or at least
lower your guard so that zombies
will kill you, so I will say no more
about my childhood. I will leave
my childhood here in this scrap
of paper like a deer in woods, hungry
and terrified of loud drunken gunshots.
I want baguettes, fromage, and real
champagne, not sparkling wine and certainly
not this sewery Columbian roast, which I
will not sentimentalize, nor will I pretend
to like having to wake to work. I just saw
a dog with a half-dead bird in its mouth.
I doubt the dog's a hero, the bird a martyr.
I'm trotting into this day with last night's
angers still in my mouth, lingering and bitter.
Did I mention the rain? The broken bottles
that I almost stepped on? The blackberries
for breakfast, stuffed into the open red wound
on the front of my face? Actually, the blackberries,
the blackberries tasted really, really right.

## Self-Portrait as a Child's Stick Figure Drawing on a Refrigerator

> "You are not what you think you are. You are something to be
> imagined."—Clayton Eshleman

Often I'm a musical instrument
that's afraid of the sounds inside.
My days consist of arrayed efforts
not to hear or hum.
I'm like a baby who screams
at first seeing his arms swinging,
unaware those whips flung
straight at his head are attached to his body.
*Why are you doing this to me?*
a man asks his body as it fights sleep
and the crucial appendage droops after a woman
says *okay, why not*, after steak and lobster
and Sandra Bullock's latest formulaic schlock.
So spent, his body mocks him; he can't
fathom how he ever lifted the long-stemmed rose
he gave her, now drooping a little bit, too.
In my son's latest drawing labeled "Daddy,"
my hairs are stray spaghetti strands,
my head an oversized triangle crushing my stick-thin frame,
and a briefcase weighs down my three-fingered hand.
Often I feel sketchy like that, as if all the wrong colors
spill over my faint lines and anyone could cross me out
just like that. I haven't always felt like a stick figure.
I haven't always been an instrument
left forgotten in its case. I remember a time
in junior high when Doug Dickerson passed me
a pornographic flip book, the male stick figure's stick penis
getting bigger and bigger and the female stick figure's
stick legs getting farther and farther apart
until the stick figure bed broke and something hidden
deep inside me broke out, broke my body wide open,
a strange inchoate music that wanted to come out.

## Confessions of a Failed Beatnik

I'll admit that I shaved my scruff, patched my jeans
and then bought slacks, and what's more, a double-breasted suit
and even shoes! matching, polished, and thus disguised,
I followed a trail of perfume that led, like a floral fluting
Pied Pieper, out of the Village, out of Manhattan even,
all the way to suburban Kentucky where I lost

myself, Man, where I forgot the words to every song
I'd ever sung to myself, let my dreams come unstitched,
Jack, quit drinking myself into nowhere Zen
stupors, and most afternoons, though not hungover,
I'm so headachy from meetings and emails
that I drive right past the brandy-colored light of

just-before sunset without pulling over to take it in,
then later rather than watching moonlight
illuminate the wind combing through unmown bluegrass,
I'm wiping kidpuke, there-there, I'm shining a flashlight
on the no-monsters under their bunk bed. I saw
the best minds of my generation toss aside their

necessary suffering, lose the art of losing, trade it all in
for golf clubs, I saw them trade the too-beautiful intensity
of feeling, feeling, feeling, for the calm comfort of
the girl-next-door's bare arms, and I'll admit I sold out, too,
and of late, no one has thought to compare me to a roman candle
exploding spider-like while everyone goes "awww!"

In fact, I mean dig this: one Fourth of July afternoon – not night –
I seared my foot on a sparkler, oh didn't I, the moral being:
don't wear sandals around any kind of lit fireworks, but
my kids were in an excited hurry so I did just that, and when
I showed them how to twirl the firey wire, a spark landed
right underneath a strap and by the time I de-sandaled, my skin

was oozing fluids, but oh listen, Cats, my left hand didn't know
what my right hand was handing it when it offered a handshake
that turned out to be really a handcuff, yes I'll admit I put all
my pot pipes and tricyclics in a box, a mildewed cardboard box
I left in front of my mortgaged tract house with "Free" written
on the side in a pungent, licorice-smelling permanent ink smear,

and I'll be the first to admit that I'm not free, that I'll change
two diapers in the time it takes you to read this, that no
odor-proof pail will keep that stench from clinging
to my memory like tobacco to clothes at a dingy tavern,
Daddy-o, and I have to admit that I rarely visit dingy taverns
because my wife hates that smell and she makes me shower

afterwards, so standing here clean-shaven and cologned
and certifiably a carpooler and little-league coach, I hereby admit,
Angels, that I disgust myself, not Robert Lowell's Peeping Tom
in "Skunk Hour" but rather Benedict Arnold of Hiptown turned
double dealing traitor, citizen of Nowheresville. No need to point
fingers or a gun to my head, Doves, I'll freely admit that most full moons

I don't howl or chase cars, because I have to work the next morning,
and I'm not the kind of cat who wears women's underwear,
I've never leapt off a bridge, put my head in an oven,
attended a bullfight, shot my wife in the head while aiming
for an apple, carved my skin and called it research,
gone to prison (except to teach a poetry class), hitched cross

country, stepped in front of a car or tank or dune buggy,
fronted a rock band, or run for office just to write about it.
I don't even keep a bride on the side or any dark secrets
except those of my friends, most of whom are characters
in forgotten novels, and because this is a confessional poem
I'll admit that I'm pee-your-pants scared of my kids.

I mean like they pretend to be ghosts and I pretend to be scared,
right? But I really am scared, pretending not to be.

Scared they'll grow up to be like me in all the wrong ways.
Scared I'll run out of bread and they'll wear secondhand
sweaters, not bohemian chic tatters but real honest-to-Buddha
hand-to-mouth, sleeping-on-storm-grates poor. Scared they won't

grow up. Scared they'll grow up and I'll grow old, quick as
a car crash, and my poems will be totaled. Scared they'll turn
me into a piano, out of tune, dust on every key.

**Road Test**

1.      Two roads diverged in a yellow wood. What did you do?
      a.      I recited Robert Frost until one road lit up like my neighbor's house at Christmas time.  I took the darker road to spite my neighbor, who borrowed and never returned my rake, and that has made all the difference
      b.      I picked the winding road, and I Kerouaced across it, Jack, oh didn't I, Daddy-O
      c.      I imagined what it must feel like to be the road, rain and sun taking turns slapping it, the lonely odor of roadkill, the ability to touch origin and destination all at once, like some crushingly-sad superhero
      d.      I did what my GPS told me to do

2.      What signs did you see along the way?
      a.      Hell is Real! on my left, Adult Books and Videos on my right, and the turn I took has made all of the difference
      b.      Washington DC or bust (in my rear view mirror, in my dust)
      c.      just the clouds, cumulus and blueblack, but with a thread of sunlight, a golden hook at the end
      d.      all of the above

3.      Did the road turn on you, darkened, potholed, a road like Cormac McCarthy's, the sun peeling the clothes off your skin and the skin off your bones?
      a.      Yes. I died with this song on my lips
      b.      Yes. I offered my bones to the vultures, quoting Robinson Jeffers: "What an enskyment! What a life after death."
      c.      No, but some bandits beat me, left me for a corpse. Some folks from my home town walked by, and now there's weirdness when I see them at Starbucks or Lowe's. Someone from the next town over stopped, called 9-1-1 for me, even visited me at the hospital, so now I

don't know how to root when our high school football teams clash

d.      No, I still have my clothes and my skin – and that has made all of the difference

4.      What did you find at the end of the road?

a.      another road, another wood, another thrill-ride for my screaming blood

b.      another false wizard who failed me

c.      no pot of gold, just some worthless junk bonds and Monopoly money

d.      I'd like to say I found myself, I found love, I found God, but I've found that to get there – to get anywhere – you've got to veer far from the straight yellow line, the paved path; you've got to make your own road and prepare to crash.

## Turning Yourself into the Wind

I know you feel like no one
knows you.  I understand
the long, disembodied slide
into the self followed by the urge
to set off car alarms and toss
a garbage lid into the street.
The good news is you're coming together
like those leaves swirling in a column
and then forming a neat mound.
But you still feel invisible, don't you?
You're still the lone citizen
of your own ravenous body.
There you go, chasing after the parts of yourself
you've felt but never found.  Bad news,
they've been watching you, the weathermen,
making their dire predictions.  They're warning
your neighbors to hide in their basements
or lie flat in a ditch somewhere,
waiting it out while you rampage and rage.
Wouldn't it feel better to turn into music
or at least into words?

## Poem On the Occasion Of

Tomorrow is our national step-barefoot-on-a-jellyfish day, so it's not a good time for tourists to visit. Unless you're coming from our enemy-state, in which case, welcome. I visited our enemy-state on their national look-up-at-the-sky day. Of course it was raining, but the subjects of our enemy-state remained stalwart. The rain in their eyes made them look like a bunch of crybabies, which they are. They've been whining ever since we stole a big chunk of their land. It was their measure-your-feet day and by the time they noticed that we had stolen their land, it was our make-new-maps-quick day and they were SOL. Contact us on our give-your-enemies-their-land-back day, we told them. When is that? they asked us. It's on your day-of-self-enforced-solitude, we told them, your day off from phones and the postal service and email and all social media. That's why we're winners and they're whiners. I wish it weren't our national step-barefoot-on-a-jellyfish day, but I won't complain because tomorrow is our national flirt-with-an-operating-room-nurse day as well as the anniversary of the day when my parents met. The day after tomorrow is penguin-awareness day, which I look forward to every year.

## Slow Dance Music

I can't explain the rain's attraction to my head,
though I'm touched by its desire to touch me.
I also can't explain unborn babies
sucking and blowing cigarettes bummed from

their young mothers, the absence of men from
the intricate inner worlds of their wives, or
the secret life of every dark street where
no one's wrist has the time. Help me

understand all the things that tumble from
the sky to the ground, from your eyes to
the corners of your mouth, from your mouth
to my ears, which are getting old, along with

the rest of me, for reasons no one has
adequately explained to me. Just when
I think I'm wearing a Tom Hunley mask
for a Halloween that never ends, I remember

that I know enough about how lost people can get,
how trapped in their own bodies and minds,
how much they resemble cattle strolling past
a huge hole in the fence, to know

I'll never understand this
music, which doesn't, after all, ask
for our understanding, only our bodies,
pressed together, swaying from side to side.

## Because You're Mine

I was shoe shopping with my wife, Jane,
the day Johnny Cash died.

I do, I like the brown strappy sandals.
As much as the silver flats?
I like them both equally, I think.
The bench is hard.  I worry
that my butt's too boney.
Beige isn't your color.  Wait, let me finish.
You somehow manage to pull it off.
I'm hungry for food court fare.
A doughy pretzel.  A bourbon chicken sample
on a toothpick.  Half off of what?
Yes, and you'll need cute new socks, sure.
Do you already own a pair of flip flops?
Definitely try those on.
The news channel, volume turned off.
His name and dates on the ticker.
A clip of him working the crowd
at Folsom Prison or San Quentin.
Those boots, the black ones, almost knee high.
What do I think?  I could die right here at Shoe Depot
in front of this mirror.
How do they feel?
Try walking the line.

## Elegy/Litany

If I describe the wind as pickpocket subtle
or as a ghost running naked through our yard,
that's called anemographia, but knowing this
won't fill my pockets or scare off the ghosts
that haunt me when the hum of our refrigerator
wakes me up.  Having my office computer stolen
woke me up to the need to always back up
files, but I'd rather move forward.  In the foreword
to a book on the Mayans, I read that our superstition
of tossing pennies into wells for good luck
has its origins in the Mayan custom of wedding virgins
to the spirit of the Well of Sacrifice.  Well.
At least I'm not a lost virgin ghost, unveiled
for some ugly well-spirit.  Last week at a $27/night hotel,
I stared at the "continental breakfast":
one banana muffin covered by a cloud of fruit flies.
I grimaced, and another hotel guest ate it, saying
"These bugs won't hurt you."  All week,
his bearded bug-eating face has haunted me.
The fear of beards is called pogonophobia.
Knowing this won't bring my laptop back
or make you love me any more.   This is an elegy
for my lost computer, but it's also an ode
to the way you can mend me with a smile or a kiss.
At Sewanee, I heard Robert Hass say all poems are either
laments, songs about ways to escape a power that can kill us,
or litanies, prayers to a power that can make us feel more alive,
and at the time, I thought that was way too reductive,
but this poem is both.  It's impossible
to put out a fire before it's been set, impossible
to scan the hard drive of my mind and eliminate
the virus that threatens to kill my memory,
impossible to save those sacrificed Mayan virgins
or say the right thing every time.
Now I can shop for a new computer.  I can

become a Luddite.  I can toss myself down a well.
But all I want to do is tell you that every love song,
every romantic movie, makes me think of you,
and no matter which way the wind blows,
it will always carry me back to you.

## While We Were on Fire, Our Shadows Glided on Water

The flames were not literal, though they
embraced like passionate drunken lovers.
We could love one another right
were it not for the pain, the throbbing pain
so strong that even saying your name
makes me want to dive deep into myself,
my cool safe shadow.  It's not our fault
that we're made of twigs is the sort
of comment that made many of my dates
turn into jellyfish instead of jelly
and so I learned that yelling "Fire"
too soon can kill a spark.  Sometimes
my life alone resembled a mountain,
not in majestic beauty but in its ability
to freeze me to death.  Sometimes I get
lost in myself as in Kafka's novels,
but love is a beast that can take any form.
Somehow I keep winding up on its back
and it carries me to you.  I didn't know
how alone I could feel until an airplane
put 3,000 miles between us.  I thought this
poem was about love but fire, water, it's about
death, about which I know even less.
Death took the poet Jack Gilbert this week,
I know that.  I sat in on a couple of his classes,
caught a couple of his readings.  He expressed
strong opinions: fans of classical music
lacked passion, tin-hearted semioticians
were stealing young minds.  He had his
graduate students write essays about the poems
of Linda Gregg, his former lover, then mailed them
to her.  A guy I used to get high with
once got drunk and smashed his knee
with a hammer, on purpose, then hobbled
into a Kroger's, knocked over a shelf,

on purpose, the purpose being to sue them.
He later vanished like April snow, and I received
the funeral announcement a week too late.
My neighbors have been putting up signs
depicting their lost cat, so she is sort of famous.
Fear flashes through their eyes, and sadness.
We're never alone.  Our pet worries keep us company.
I have more worries than I have words for them,
but mostly I worry that I'll lose you and wander
around my dark, cluttered self without a cat's night vision.
Jack Gilbert wrote poems about carrying
his grief over the death of Michiko, another lover,
about finding locks of her hair weeks after
the funeral.  I thought this poem was about death
but it's about separation, those three weeks last summer
spent across the ocean from you, how I feared
that the distance would kill me.

## Prelude to Pillow Talk

From the pipes, from the TV, noises gathered, grew.
　Chekhov wrote that sexy women are sexier when
they pretend not to notice you, I said, which wasn't true.
　It wasn't Chekhov, but rather our alcoholic friend
one night when the tides were in, their wisdom washing
　over and through him. She sat straight, silent,
like a metronome waiting for the real music to start.
　Our living room, full of kid-toys, looked like
a deconsecrated church, but I didn't say so. I didn't
　want to speak at all, or listen, but I did listen
when she said our life is a DVR filled with kid-shows,
　out of memory. Then a silence set in our stomachs
until she said I feel swallowed up like the smallest
　nesting doll, and I, searching for something new
to say, found only Fo'shizzle. Chekhov did say that
　if there's a shotgun on stage, it must go off before
curtains fall, by which I think he meant this poem needs
　to return to our alcoholic friend. He introduced us
to each other, without which, there never would have been
　pillow talk between us, certainly no kid-toys, no stain
on our carpet where he passed out last summer, tipping over
　a bottle of hot sauce. We worry about him, sure,
like we worry about our kids, and that worry sits between us
　unsure of what it is, how it got here. The November light
strained through our window blinds, and the sad beauty
　of orange-yellow-red leaves stabbed me. The sad beauty
of orange-yellow-red leaves stabs me, I said. Fo'shizzle,
　she said. And your beauty too, I said, it stabs me
in the heart. That's a stain from my gushing blood, not
　from hot sauce, I said, and she gave me a look that said
you big dork.

## Elizabeth Taylor's White Diamonds

Eggo Waffles give me the willies
even more than crepes.  I can handle
eggs if they're not devilled, scrambled, or
especially sunny-side up, which always reminds me that
eventually the sun will burn out or
else an asteroid will collide with our sweet
earth.  Breakfast always takes me to the
edge of the tallest, darkest cliff, from which only
espresso can ever pull me back with its
eerie gravity, its strange scent –
extra strong, like my wife's perfume, which I searched for
everywhere before we finally met, which I
experience,
every night, as a magic
elixir that makes the day's troubles
evaporate.

## Yellow Poem

It's true what the yellowed Cold War
newspaper said about missiles ready
and eager to shatter the mountains
at Yellowstone National Park.  It's true, too,
that I have to search three sets of yellow pages
for the number of the receptionist
who books appointments for the dental assistant
who will help me white out the yellow coffee stains
on my teeth.  And of course it's true that I must
be ready for whatever might befall this world
full of marigolds and canaries and drugged-out
blonde models, not to mention the yet-unpublished
young, still green, with a readiness and an eagerness
to inherit my loneliness, my emptiness,
coursing through them.  Nevertheless,
I can't get over this curled mass of messy yarn,
yellow in a cat's teeth, yellow like a cat's teeth.
I'm so grateful for this sunlight
that I could, and why don't I? fly a kite
with a picture of a banana on it, a kite
made from a print of the original artwork
for my favorite album, *The Velvet Underground & Nico*.

## VC

I just tripped on bamboo in Trung's backyard.
It snapped, not too loud, but loud enough
for him to catch me. We're eleven, playing "VC"
with his four brothers. VC is like Tag,
but if you're "it," you have to pretend
to be the Viet Cong. It's my turn
to be the Viet Cong, but first Trung wants
to tell me something broken and jungledark.
His brothers' laughter betrays their hiding places.
I don't have the heart to find them.

Trung tells me about his sister wailing,
looking back home, looking ready to turn into salt;
about their father's slap on her cheek
followed by a caress on the red spot.
The seasick boat rocks and awaits them.
The latenight air is chilly.

Half of Trung's brothers have peed themselves.
I'm the Viet Cong, and I can almost smell it.
Ten years later, Trung and I smoke some strong
stinky weed together on break from our different
colleges, and I lose him in the haze. I look
on Facebook and in the phone book.
I'll never find him.

## No One to Ask for Directions

Do those patches of forest
untouched by man
ever get lonely or
lost inside themselves
with no notion of maps,
no one to ask for directions?
Snow-covered ground no one
ever sees can do anything it wants.
The sun will never know.
Then there's us, melting snowmen
trying to keep the pipes in our mouths
and the noses on our faces,
trying to hold it all in.

## Inside the Belly

When the light strikes your face
at just the right angle, I can almost
see our future, all bright and shiny
in your eyes is something I heard
Rufus say five times in the same evening
to different women with the same
results.  I don't know anyone
named Rufus, but I hope he
finally made it, found happiness,
grew into his body, which was clumsy
and slow like a John Deere tractor
bringing traffic to a grinding halt
is the first verse of a song I heard
on my car stereo during a road trip
past the corn fields of Indiana.  Do you
believe there are angels whose whole job
is to salvage all the fragments,
all our half-finished efforts?
Where was I?  Oh right, Indiana.
It swallowed me up because I said
I'll be damned before I move to Kentucky
I heard a preacher say while he
lassoed a snake above his head.
Something I ate had poisoned me.
I was starting to feel it.  My stomach
testified, and a perfumed woman in
a large straw hat shouted Amen.

## An Afternoon in a Children's Story

The doctor diagnosed Rachel as
a contestant on a game show.
"No wonder I feel twittery
as if jolted by a buzzer and the gasps
of a studio audience shooting through
my whole body," she said as the doctor
prescribed that she shake her ass
from side to side, the way a donkey
swishes its tail to fight flies.
Obviously that doctor was a quack
and a lech. All she needed was
to change the channel. That and a map
of the world inside this world.
A map to help her navigate the suffering.
Sadly, our cartographers have busied themselves
showing all the places people have thrown TVs
out windows and making computer models
to predict the next launch. Rachel walked
into Best Buy, where her friend Nathan worked
every day despite threatening, every night,
to quit. "I'd like to buy a vowel,"
she told him. "I really would," and he said
he'd check in the back. They had twenty
TVs, all showing *Alice in Wonderland,* and
Rachel watched them all, feeling like a baby
fly seeing the world for the first time.
"This is the only map I'll ever need,"
she said, transfixed. "Off with her head,"
said the Queen. "Take this job and
give it to someone else," said Nathan,
hoisting a forty-two inch flat screen
over his head. "I'll throw this
through the window. I'll do it."

## Big News
### (After Tomaz Salamun)

Tom Hunley is one of the wild things
from *Where the Wild Things Are.*
Tom Hunley is the home run ball
people bite each other over in the cheap seats.
His favorite time of day is twilight, of course,
when everything is happening. Other people
and I, we pat him on the back when he walks by.
We buy him drinks. Why not? The world
is getting heavy with so many people
eating so many Big Macs, and sometimes
Tom Hunley acts like Atlas said
"Hold this" and then "Sucka!"

It used to be he could fly, they say,
but ex-girlfriends and other detractors
plucked his wings and showed them to him.
It used to be he could see, too, but
ex-girlfriends and other detractors plucked
his eyes, and for a second, he swears,
he could see himself perfectly.
This is all figurative, of course.
Tom Hunley taught that distinction
and so many others to me
and to so many others.

I've been following Tom Hunley on Twitter.
Today he's in Bowling Green, Kentucky.
Next week, maybe Fairmont, Minnesota,
City of Lakes. You can waterski there,
or snowmobile, and *don't forget your fishing pole!*
says Randy Quiring, Mayor. Next week
Tom Hunley and his sons plan to fly
a box kite in Fairmont, Minnesota,
and it will be big news there,

the wildest thing to hit Fairmont, Minnesota since the grasshopper infestation of 1873.

## Shallow

The water rose only to his knees.
He came to swim so he swam,
his knees scraping the cement pool floor.
He could see the dull green paint.
Someone had left a penny down there.
He would never scoop up a penny
in a parking lot or from the aisle
of a supermarket, but he dove after this one.
It slipped through his fingers
and down the drain. He thought maybe
he wouldn't bother to come up for air.
He knew his problems were only
a foot deep. People were starving
other people, making them listen
to Christina Aguilera CDs really loud
in sleep-deprived states. It didn't matter.
A kitten can scratch your eyes and somehow
that's more terrible than if a tiger does it.

## Where My Name Comes From

A plaque above my writing desk says
Thomas means *seeker of truth*
but the truth is that Thomas means *twin*,
according to Linda Rosencrantz,
author of *The Very Last Word on First Names*,
whose first name means "the one who is waiting"
and whose last name she shares
with one of Hamlet's friends who famously
dies offstage.  I got the name from
my mother, who got it from my father,
before their marriage died offstage.
I have a son named Blake Thomas,
after William Blake, the writer and painter;
James Blake, the tennis player; my father;
myself; and Dylan Thomas, who named
one of his books *Portrait of the Artist as a Young Dog*
and drank himself to death, which
I tried to do when I was younger,
succeeding only in killing my unhappy twin.
Had he survived, he would be forty today
and I don't think he would recognize me.

## Poem For April Snow

Up in the air, a gust hoisted a piece
of paper with the great poem on it
that this poem wants to be just like.
This poem has heard me murmuring,
in my disturbed sleep, about the great poem
the wind ripped away from me.
All I remember about that great poem
are the words "April Snow." This poem
heard me murmuring those words like
a dying man muttering "Rosebud,"
which is what I might name my sled
if an April snow were to appear outside
my window, where right now there's only
sunlight glistening on my neighbor's roof,
a bird I don't know the name of,
and a girl I don't know the name of
riding a bike I don't know the name of,
though I've decided to call the bike Huffy
and the girl April Snow. April Snow, eat lots
of Sweet Tarts before your metabolism slows
and the world tells you to hate your body.
Eating Sweet Tarts will help you understand
this world, which is sweet and tart, often
at the same time, safely dangerous like the park
where your Huffy is carrying you. You will drift
in and out of so many places, if you're like me.
I named you after a spring snowstorm
that surprised me ten years ago in Denver,
which I visited without checking with
the weatherman. Even if you check
with the weatherman, April Snow, you might
get caught in an April snow. Weather forecaster,
I mean. You could be the one everyone turns to
for help making plans, but they might not
appreciate hearing the truth: that life is uncertain.

Try to enjoy the tarts as well as the sweets.
Watch out for cars whose drivers aren't
watching out, April Snow, and for strangers
in the park with hands full of Sweet Tarts.
*Climb onto the ledge*, the ledge may whisper.
The park is haunted but only because it's full
of people who are haunted.  You pedaled away
while I wrote this poem, and now there's a white
squirrel rooted to the spot where I first saw you.
This poem tells me that you haven't gone
anywhere, that you've turned into that white squirrel.
That's what I've been trying to tell you,
what this poem has been trying to tell me.
The world moves fast from nice calm sky
to ice storm, however reassured you and I
might be by rhymes like "girl" and "squirrel."

## Thaw

*I'm hungry*, I told the frozen pizza,
and to the windstorm I said,
*You're from Chicago?  My friend*
*moved there to avoid herself,* which
I can understand, though mostly I'm
speeding towards myself
hoping only to avoid a collision.
I have felt like a furniture sale where
everything must go, you know, before
the arson, and also like the droopy flower
that ruined the whole arrangement
and made the bride cry.  I've seen pigeons
staggering in shadows cast by pine trees,
and I've seen drunks ambulating
towards bathrooms in taverns pitch black
except for the lamps above pool tables.
I try to hang on as long as I can,
like the icicles hanging onto office awnings
above the heads of smokers.  I've felt at times
like a balloon running out of helium, a car
running out of gas, a pizza box emptied of all
but the crusts.  And now, early in my
forty-second February, I feel like
a snowman, as if tomorrow I'll be nothing
but a carrot, a pipe, and ashes where two
charcoal eyes sat before somebody squirted them
with lighter fuel and struck a match.

## Sphinx on a Leash

*After Jean Arp*

Tell me where the wind carries the aroma
of my wife's cream cheese brownies when she
bakes with the window open.  And tell me, what color
best approximates the fear that blows through my sons
as the emboldened wind pushes back the curtains
and sings the song of its gathering strength?

Will the people I know most always remain
mysteries to me, Sphinx?  I'm 500 miles from them,
watching news of a tornado.  Today thirteen people
have been blown out of Kentucky into the unknown
next world or into nothingness.  Don't tell me which.
I'm not ready to know.

You've got to do what I say, Sphinx, or I'll yank
on this leash until you yelp.  Tell me my loved ones
are safe, laughter floating over their heads.  Tell me
I'll see them tomorrow, or I'll tell you, as you once
told Oedipus, that your father is a dead man
and that you can go fuck your mother.

## Listen, a Wave Crashing Against a Cage with a Petty Thief and an Angel Inside It

I think I hear a shuffling deck or
leaves torn by swirls of wind and rain.
I can feel gravity, which brings me
down, Man.  I can feel the vanishing
work of the hours moving across
the gray streets like a virus for which
we have no immunization.
Ladies and Gentlemen of my
Tenure Review Board, consider
my dissertation on the number
of angels that glow and then fade
on the tip of a chosen, blessed
blade of grass.  No one has cited it,
nor has anyone refuted it.  Consider also
the thief who specializes in hubcaps,
VW emblems, spoilers, and headlights
because he is an artist who believes in
art's ability to transport us, which is to
say he's an angel, unconstrained by time
and social conventions such as the law,
but justice being what it is, he works
now without any sunlight, with no music
to carry him along but the damaged,
raspy hum of this poem, which made him
then made him steal in the name of art
which failed to find a way out for him,
failed to put wings on him to let him
lift off, which left him nothing but a deck
of cards, every hand a bad one.

## Eight Bits Usually Equals One Byte

A cracking voice asks, *Is this English 100?*
I look up at this string-thin, patchy-bearded kid
resembling Shaggy just after tumbling out of
the Mystery Machine, spooked, certain his dog can talk.
I tell him, *Yes, but this is the fourth week; you've already
flunked,* and he flies out of the room so fast
he may as well be the snowball that flattened
on the statued bust that I passed on my way to class.
Sometimes I wish I could hide in the darkness
inside my shirt pocket. *Where is the professor?*
*He was just here, and there's his shirt.*

I don't know the etymology of the statement
*The quarterback drops back into the pocket,*
but if my OED can't tell me, my computer will.
Ditto the difference between *flotsam* and *jetsam*
and between *hem* and *haw,* and between *bits* and *bytes,*
but no dictionary or computer can tell me how my student,
Willie McNeal, feels today, or whether I did right
by that *Is this English 100?* kid.  Last week
Willie was the chain-sporting, diamond-studded hero
who had run a kickoff back for a touchdown. This week
he's the bruised, black-eyed kid who lost his grip

on the game-winning touchdown pass. All week
he drifts back and forth between English class and his dreams,
too tired from suicide sprints to stay awake.  I don't need
a dictionary or a computer to understand the term *suicide sprints,*
but *flotsam* refers to shipwrecked goods spilled into the water,
like Willie if he doesn't get up after the next hit,
and *jetsam* signifies goods voluntarily tossed overboard
or jettisoned, like that *Is this English 100?* kid.
*Hem* and *haw* come from *ahem* and an old form of *huh,*
and they work together, like a quarterback and receiver in sync,
who do not hem and haw, but strike with no fear of failure.

Class, a poet named Keats said we should write about mysteries,
uncertainties, and doubts without any irritable reaching
after fact, and then he got TB and died at twenty-six.
Also I thought someone threw a snowball across the street
this morning, but it was a leaping white squirrel
and someone's hosing its guts off her Goodyear tires right now.
All of you floated in here today filled with fears
and feelings you can't name. They follow you
as surely as shadows, all the way past the edge of where your
parents and teachers can go with you, and sometimes I think of you
as bits and bytes in programming code infected with a virus
or as new words that haven't yet entered the dictionary.

## Death and Other Dirty Jokes

For years I went to AA meetings and told the same
stories, puffed-up with streetwise bravado:
the time I sat on a departing city bus and watched
through the window while my drug dealer was
held up at knife point, the time I woke up shirtless

on a stranger's lawn, the time 1 drunk-dialed
the previous night's first date from the steel-barred
city drunk tank. None of these stories were lies,
but, as Melville wrote in *Billy Budd*, "Truth
uncompromisingly told, will always have its

ragged edges," and my ragged truth was so much
more pathetic and dull: walking for miles in
Seattle rain without bus fare, collecting beer bottles
in my sister's basement, missing class and giving
the same old excuses, hollow as worn-out jokes

that weren't funny in the first place, like the one
about growing up so poor my mama cut holes
in my pockets so I'd have something to play with.
I repeated that groaner over and over to my eye-rolling
wife, not knowing where I'd first heard it, until

my uncle—whom I hadn't seen for thirty years –
told it at my grandpa's funeral. Those wasted years,
I like to think I was a forgotten Stratocaster trapped in its case,
but in truth, I think I was Esau, unable to see
past the edges of my hunger and the steaming bowl

of stew. I was a stupid kid, eager to toss away his life.
Grandpa, I barely knew you. I know you hand-crafted clocks,
worked for Standard Oil for like forty years, and loved
your 1960 Studebaker. I'm pretty sure you never
wore makeup outside of the coffin. I know you

got old, and now I want to know what that's like. Tell me,
have you heard any good jokes lately? Tell me about
those last coughing fits, the fight to keep your soul
from bursting out of your body like a blurt or a fart.
Tell me something crude and coarse and side-splittingly true.

## Ode to Being a Wreck

You remind me that I live
in this world, which is a junkyard,
and that naturally you live in me
or at least you keep a time share
in me where you vacation when
others evict you because they
have it all sorted out.  You save me
from believing too much in myself.
You remind me that I'm a moon,
not a planet.  Usually I don't even
feel inhabitable, which is okay
for a sometime misanthrope.
Being a Wreck, I could kiss you.
You were there -- and you were
the only one -- when I woke hungover
in someone else›s car and couldn't
find my own.  You were there when
my back went out from under me
and the dishes piled up as I watched
you through the glaze of painkillers.
You were there when I straightened
my hair, Scope-sprayed my breath,
and tried to ask Jane out for the first time,
my voice muffled like I had a mouthful
of spinach.  And you were there later when
I heard another man talking on Jane›s voicemail.
I'm not strong like Popeye, Being a Wreck.
He's a classic cartoon.  I'm a minor character
in a WB dramedy.  I'm the joke that God
began telling before forgetting the punchline.
I need Him to remember me, which He
won't do until you arrive, Being a Wreck,
like a tiger in the rushes or like The Misfit
in that Flannery O'Connor story, pointing
a gun at me to teach me how to pray.

## Villanelle on Two Lines by Bill Knott

(Collaboration with Denise Duhamel)

I know there is something lost
like my girlfriend, the blond—
as if to say, what I have least

wanted is what I've gotten, at first, at last.
True, towards the end she was bland,
but I know there is something lost

and I will fight to get it back, lest
she and I be blind—
as if to say, what I have least

wanted to reveal, you've seen, my guts and lust
all swirling in a blender.
I know there is something lost

and forgotten or cut away from every list,
my masks and murders, blimps and blunders—
as if to say, what I have leased,

what I have taken, what has been laced,
what I have blown. Duh.
I know there is something lost
as if to say, what I have least.

## Questionnaire

Have you ever been treated
unfairly or for depression?
Have you ever been cheated

in tennis, told to remain seated,
disciplined, pinned, discipled, or shunned?
Have you ever been treated

like water treats flame, told you're unneeded,
made to feel foreign?
Have you ever been cheated

out of a week's wages, greeted
on the street by your old lover and her new one?
Have you ever been treated

for drug addiction, imprisoned, defeated
by a badge and a gun?
Have you ever been cheated

in strip poker? Have you ever seceded
from a union? Can we trust you with our son
and our money? Have you ever been treated
like this? Have you ever been cheated?

## Thanksgiving Psalm

God gave us stuff
God stuffed us
Give thanks
to God
Stuff turkeys to
stuff us
Thanks God
Thanks turkeys
Give turkey
back to God
God give us enough
stuff
Stuff us
God
God stuffs us turkeys
with Godstuff
Let there be
stuff
God said
Thanks God
and there was
stuff was
God there
God was
God suffered
enough
for us
Thanks God
for giving us enough
forgiving us
for stuff

## Scotch Tape World

Taping my thigh and calf together
at the knee, I contemplate taking
my children to Scotch Tape World,
where stars fall from the sky
like posters from my office door, where
the tires could fly off our car at
any moment.  It's time they learn
that life is like that, that Disney lies
in the way of a true education.  God
never lies, but He's still in trouble.
Why else would He have to clean
all the blackboards on which we
are math problems and incorrect sums?
Our prayers go to Heaven, but first they go
through Scotch Tape World.  Torn in transport,
they're pieced back together and presented
to God, who receives them as music
rather than as words.  Holding your breath
waiting for people to be decent is one way
to go to God, who loves us just as He loves
the notes that David's harp wrote to Him.
Low clouds overhead seem to come
apart as if held together by cheap Scotch
tape.  Such a pointless death, like the one
suffered by my first car, not to mention
Kenneth Patchen, who wrote "The animal
I wanted couldn't get into the world" and
other lines penned, as Valery said, "by someone
other than the poet to someone other than
the reader."  Our prayers might be missives
from someone other than us to someone
other than God.  Behind my beard is a face
that's different from the one my wife married
years ago.  Behind any given joke is the funk
that made us look for laughter.  If you don't

know what I mean, you'll wake up one day
knowing.  You'll look up and see sunlight hitting
a mountain so hard they both seem ready to shatter.

## The House of Hunley

"I will call this plant/ bougainvillea, exclaims Bogainville/ upon discovering
what the natives formerly called/ ass weed."
—Jason Bredle, "Wild Animals You Never Knew You Could Eat"
(*A Twelve Step Guide: Poems*)


The House of Bourbon ruled Europe
  for centuries, but do we remember
    their laws, their names, their restoration
      to power after the bloody French Revolution?
In most of our houses, they're not remembered
  at all, though we invoke their names at AA meetings
    or when supping the corn mash elixir that teaches us
      how to forget, all because French-speaking
        settlers sought to honor them by christening
          their new Kentucky home Bourbon County.

Had Oedipus existed, I'm sure he would have wanted
  to be remembered as Oedipus the King,
    rather than Oedipus the Motherfucker,
      his indelible legacy, thanks to Sophocles and Freud.

I have three sons who will carry on my name.
This morning the three-year-old beat me
  at a Superhero Squad memory game,
    and last week the five-year-old said "The earth
      is bigger than anything on earth."
Surely my legacy is safe with them.
The seven-year-old, who loves vacuum cleaners
  and bought one with his own allowance, wraps
    the cord around his shoulders like a guitar strap and strums.
Someday someone may say, So-and-So really Hunleyed the Hell
  out of that guitar, or So-and-So belongs in the guitar pantheon
    with Hendrix and Page and Clapton and Hunley.

But I can't control that any more than Bernard Lewinsky
  could control the wildfire spread of the term

"getting a Lewinsky."
Bernard, an oncologist, has probably saved
thousands of lives, but all we remember about him
are his daughter's visits to the oval office.

The name Jean Nicot lives on, not because
as French Ambassador to Portugal in 1659,
he arranged the marriage of a French princess
to the Portugese king, but because he introduced
the tobacco plant to Europe.

I want, more than anything, to be remembered for my poems,
any of my poems, even those tucked near the back of my books.
I swear I won't whine, like Anthony Burgess, boo-hooing
because the book that made him rich and famous,
*A Clockwork Orange*, just wasn't his best book.
I won't whine *why why won't anyone read the others?*

I just want a small bite of immortality, that luscious fruit
that has tantalized humans since Genesis Three.
And when I say "tantalized," you should know I'm invoking the name
of Tantalus, who stole nectar and ambrosia and tried to feed
his own child to the gods, for which Zeus placed him
up to his chin in water, beneath a tempting, teasing fruit tree,
its branches just out of reach.

## Still Life with Laugh Track

is a clever title, I suppose.  It got you
reading.  I hope I don't lose you.
Whether you've lost your umbrella or a bout
with a UFC badass or with terminal
grandiosity or even if you're the thing
that's been lost, listen, I know it's strange,
under these circumstances, to think
of giving your dog a bath, or your child,
or even your tired, begrimed self.

As I get older, it gets easier to fall
asleep in a chair and to fly into myself
in that captain-of-a-private-plane position.
*I am the tacit light of the stars*, wrote Paul Guest
in a poem I quite like and I'm happy
for him, but if I'm a light
why can't anyone near me read
or see where they're going?

How do I know my child
isn't right about the darkness
having monsters all over it?
What if a man is at once a monster
under the bed and a child clinging
to his second-favorite stuffed animal
because his favorite is lost like a
whisper no one will ever hear?

## Paranoid Love Song

As if I've never seen you smile at my
friends right in front of my face, which I
straightened with all my strength.
As if I weren't receiving daily phone calls
from my future self warning me of potholes
that I step in anyway because how do I know
my future self isn't fucking with me?
I know myself, and it's the kind of thing
I'd do. As if I could be king and you
could be queen, which David Bowie promised
but did he mean you and me?
Who's been calling your cell, verse one.
Your hand on my best friend's knee,
come on and admit it, verse two.
As if I say all this to you and you say
as if. As if I was a werewolf but now
I'm Scott again, and I say *I'm sorry
I about bit your head off back there.*
As if I could become your pet parrot and call
your new boyfriend *Cracker*, his penis *peanut*.
As if my heart darkened and you opened
the window blinds to make a sunlight square
to soak it in. As if you would ever leave me
for Richard Dawson. He kisses every female
*Family Feud* contestant. When I close my eyes
all I see are fruit flies. When they close their eyes
all they see is garbage. The garbage truck comes
with screeching brakes while they're sleeping
and they wake bereft. Buzzing and banging heads
against screen doors. Like me after the inevitable
bull comes charging at me. After you've left.

## A Little Less Beauty

The girl that I loved saw the moon in a lake
She thought it was the real moon but it was a fake
She was drunk and she hugged that shimmering light
She went down and she drowned and her body didn't fight
Never again will I touch the body of that girl
Now there's a little less beauty in this world

I think I see her face but it's in my mind
I think I hear her voice but it's just the wind
I know I should forget her but I can't forget her
Sometimes I wish I'd never met her

I made that girl up to show you how it feels
to have the kind of heart that breaks and never heals
I made the girl up but the feeling is real
Now there's less beauty less spice in each meal
Never again will I touch the body of that girl
Now there's a little less beauty in this world

## And Suddenly It's Evening

*after Salvatore Quasimodo*

The sky is perfect, like new.
A flock of birds lifts off. You watch,
and when your eyes return to earth,
you see a lipsticked, dimpled smile.
You hear a skirt fluttering in the wind
like a flag you long to salute,
and it is your own beating heart.
You see legs you pretend not to see.
The young woman with wild
brunette hair giggles and asks you
for a light. You think maybe, it seems
possible, she really wants more.
You blink. The sky darkens.
You become wrinkled and bald.
The young woman with wild
brunette hair says "pardon me, sir,"
steps around you, asks a frat boy
to light her cigarette.

## Where All the Streets Lead in Every Direction

And so, with nowhere to go, half-awake,
I keep on walking in both worlds
on the pavement that sends heat
up my pantlegs.  And so, the job gets done,
the paycheck signed, but what I do for
the money and what I do with the money
seem to have nothing to do with one another.
Like my parents who still won't sit in the same
room after all these stretched years.
Unseen, unknown parts of me gather and
alight all at once like a flock of birds, so
why can't I get close enough to anyone
or far away enough from everyone?
People brush against me on crosswalks,
which sometimes feels nice like sunlight
but always makes me check on my wallet,
a reflex.  And then, hooray!  You can
go around licking people's hearts, but you'll
poison your own while inviting stares.
It takes practice to walk a straight line
after the sky darkens.  My body remembers
and is afraid that no one's following it.  Yes,
I can give you directions, replete with landmarks,
but I'll be making it up as I go.

## P.S. and P.P.S.

"Writing a poem is like catching a fish." —William Stafford

I.

Often in a crowd I feel like I'm in a car wash
but I forgot my car, and I'm getting drenched
and broken or worse, I feel like the nickel
on the carpet that no one picks up because
it's not paper money. By now everyone
with anywhere to be has gone there
in their blue Trans Ams and good riddance.
There's only enough room in these rooms for
a few heads wondering how anyone deals with
three score and ten, even a life spent in cozy
American suburbia, only enough room, and
barely enough, for a few hearts willing to feel
the whole unbearable weight of the truth
about themselves. The truth is in my dreams,

II.

I am a fish drawn irresistibly
to a wormy hook, and I wake,
kind of flopping around
with a moth on my tongue.
The first time I was in love I thought
I was in the ocean, but really I was
in a bucket, and when I was thrown back
for being too small, I missed the hook
in my mouth, and it was hard
to breathe during my freefall.
Dear Everyone Who Stayed This Long,
I almost forgot to tell you
I once caught a fish that was This Big.
I cooked it up, it fed me, and I saved some for you.

## My Worst Fear Comes True

They change the English language, entirely,
while I sleep, announcing it bilingually
(Tom's English and New English)
on a social networking site
I don't know about. My job
as an English teacher is in peril.
If I say, *Do you have the time?* or
*I'll have a double latte, please*, the reply
might be *lightning hours* or *grey wind*.

I misread people's faces
because they've changed
body language, too.
Middle finger if you want the ketchup passed.
Pee dance upon greeting, instead of a handshake.

When I say *I love you*
to my beautiful wife
she calls the cops, because
those words no longer
mean what they used to mean.
A bilingual cop urges me to take
ESL and Body Language for Nobodies.
Instead of saying *I love the way your hair smells
and the sound of your breathing*, he instructs me
to say *avocado treefrog, honeyed sunlight*.
Instead of leaning in for a kiss, he says
I should use an old gang handshake, now used
by umpires to signal *safe at home*.

# Acknowledgements

Some of these poems have been previously published, as indicated below.

*Anti-*: "Um"

*Atlanta Review*: "Turning Yourself Into the Wind"

*Atticus Review:* "Eight Bits Usually Equals One Byte," "Speaking of Falls," "Speechless Like Michael Cain"

*Catch Up*: "No One to Ask for Directions"

*Diode Poetry Journal*: "Wives of the Poets," "Elegy/Litany," "At the Afterlife Bar and Grill"

*The Fiddleback*: "Death and Other Dirty Jokes"

*Ithaca Lit*: "Questionnaire" and "And Suddenly It's Evening"

*Leveler Poetry:* "Inside the Belly"

*Louisville Review*: "Permanent" and "Poem for April Snow"

*MARGIE*: "Big News" and "Where My Name Comes From"

*Mojave River Review:* "Blurbs"

*National Poetry Review*: "Self-Portrait as a Child's Stick Figure Drawing on a Refrigerator"

*New Orleans Review*: "Slow Dance Music"

*New South*: "Thaw"

*New Southerner*: "The House of Hunley".

*North American Review*: "Moonhandled"

*Open 24 Hours*: "Prelude to Pillow Talk"; "Listen, a Wave Crashing Against a Cage With an Angel and a Petty Thief Inside It"; and "What If There Lives, Within You, A Man Who Loves Random Consolations?"

*Paddlefish*: "Confessions of a Failed Beatnik"

*Perspectives*: "Psalm on a Theme by Dean Young and a Somewhat Similar Theme by Allen Ginsberg," and "Thanksgiving Psalm"

*Ping Pong*: "Sphinx on a Leash"

*Poems & Plays*: "My Worst Fear Comes True"

*Rosebud*: "Road Test"

*Route Seven Review*: "Another Dream of Falling"

*The Scream*: "Scotch Tape World"

*Valparaiso Poetry Review*: "Um"

*Verse Daily*: "Slow Dance Music," "Scotch Tape World," "Self-Portrait as a Child's Stick Figure Drawing on a Refrigerator"

*Verse Wisconsin*: "Psalm on a Theme by Dean Young and a Somewhat Similar Theme by Allen Ginsberg"

*The Volta*: "Big News"

*Windhover: A Journal of Christian Literature*. "Eight Bits Usually Equals One Byte"

*The Writer*: "Villanelle on Two Lines by Bill Knott"

*Zone 3*: "What Can Be Said about the Beautiful-from-a-Distance Elegant Etcetera in the Broken Syllables of Our Imperfect Tongues?"

The following people read and critiqued earlier, more embarrassing drafts of this manuscript, and I am deeply indebted to them: Brent Fisk, Jeannine Hall Gailey, Joshua Johnston, Molly McCaffrey, Jeff Newberry, April Ossman, and Austin Segrest. The book's title was Eduardo Corral's suggestion, and he also generously offered to write a blurb, which I appreciated even though I declined. Thanks also to the others who offered to blurb this book: Dave Essinger, Stacia Flegal, John Guzlowski, Saeed Jones, and Gabriel Welsch. This book and my life are dedicated to Ralaina.

# About the Author

Tom C. Hunley is a professor of English at Western Kentucky University, the director of Steel Toe Books, and the vocalist/rhythm guitarist for Dr. Tom and the Cartoons. He is the author of three previous full-length poetry collections, two textbooks, and six chapbooks. He is the co-editor, with Alexandria Peary, of *Creative Writing Pedagogies for the Twenty-First Century*, forthcoming from Southern Illinois University Press. He divides his time between Kansas and Oz.